BONE APPÉTIT!

Natural Foods for Pets

by Frances Sheridan Goulart

PACIFIC
Search BOOKS
715 Harrison Street
Seattle, Washington 98109

Cover and Book Design by Marilyn Weber
Illustrated by Marilyn Weber

Copyright© 1976 by Pacific Search Books
International Standard Book Number 0-914718-17-7
Library of Congress Catalog Card Number 76-40370
Manufactured in the United States of America

Contents

*This one is
for Bemsha, Dimsun,
the late Budwig, and
all of my other
dear departed
four-footed friends.*

Introduction

The time has come to bite the biscuit.

Our pets, like the rest of us, should be eating a bit lower on the hog and a lot higher on the peanut.

Man's best friend consumes 175 pounds of meat and meat by-products each year while man's other best friend, the cat, puts away 150 pounds of manufactured, meaty delicacies. (According to one major manufacturer of pet foods, fifty cents of every dollar spent on cat food is spent on "luxury cat food," meaning a meal containing top quality kidney, beef liver, ground beef, etc.)

Is all this expense and animal protein strictly necessary? And rising costs aside, what about the chemicals in your chow chow's chow? Last but not least, what about the psychological benefits of an occasional home-cooked meal? Who's to say how well Bowser and Puss live by bone and by-product alone?

Bone Appétit! therefore says, if you're going to the dogs (and sixty percent of the households in America have)*, do it with a homemade handout that's the cat's meow. *Bone Appétit!* offers just that—a collection of wholesome homespun supplements for your pet's store-bought rations plus snacks that are simple and inexpensive with low or no animal protein.

New cat and dog days are upon us. The time has come not only to bite the biscuit, but to bake it as well.

Bone Appétit!

---

*According to *Time* magazine, there are about 100 million cats and dogs in American households ("The Great American Animal Farm," *Time*, 23 December 1974, 58).

Boning Up:

Ingredients

WHOLE GRAINS It is best to buy whole grains and grind them into meal, cracked grain, and flour as you need them. You can even make your own fresh bran flakes (see index). Flour is incredibly quick to spoil (oxidation is well under way in eighteen hours, in even less time with wheat germ), but whole grains keep virtually forever and can be sprouted. You will probably want to have some if not all of the following on hand. There are also convenient blends of nuts, seeds, and grains sold as twelve- or seven-grain cereals, etc., at your health food store.

Most domesticated carnivorous animals depend on cereals for all their essential minerals as well as the majority of vitamins, including the fertility vitamin E, found in the germ of grains, especially wheat. If flaked, cereals can be served raw. In addition to wheat:

Oats: A good source of iron, an aid in proper cleansing of the intestines, and the stuff on which many of Great Britain's famed collie dogs have been reared. Look to porridge for stamina and resistance to infections.

Barley: Like rice, a very old and venerable grain. And similar to rice, it is a source of calcium and magnesium and is readily digested. Makes a good cup of canine tea, too.

Rice: Contains all eight of the essential amino acids, has a not-to-be-sniffed-at amount of the B-vitamin niacin, and if you use only brown rice, you get a bonus. Grind it for flour and what is left in the sifter is rice bran, a B-vitamin-rich supplement for your dog's or cat's next repast.

Rye: Contains more protein than rice and what else is right nice about rye is that it makes good dog biscuits that have the minerals manganese, phosphorus, and potassium. Hearty, and sprouts well in cool weather.

Corn: Corn oil is especially valuable as a moisturizer for dry food. Degerminated cornmeal helps to grow beautiful and abundant hair and strong teeth.

Millet: Perhaps the most alkaline of all grains, millet resembles corn in color but is more minute and has a taste rather like undomesticated or wild corn (if there were such a thing). Somewhat lower in calories and carbohydrates than corn, it is referred to here as "mock cornmeal." Also try buckwheat (or kasha), couscous, and cracked wheat for variety.

NUTS AND SEEDS Even in small quantities, nuts and seeds are sources of the B-vitamins, many of which are removed in the processing of commercial pet foods. Seeds should always be used raw, unseasoned, and unhulled. In their sprouted form, they are even better body builders.

VEGETABLES Onions and garlic are favored by most pets for curious curative powers in the face of numerous ailments. Curative or not, they can contribute some vitamins, minerals, and roughage, especially if eaten raw and finely chopped or prepared with a minimal amount of processing. (Cats are said to favor spinach, string beans, carrots, and turnips. Dogs, in general, are fond of cabbage, carrots, peas, onions, lima beans, and turnips.)

SPROUTS Sprouts make a perfect pooch hootch for your pet, since they are vitamin and mineral enriched. Put ¼ cup whole grains (wheat, rye, oats, etc.) into a large wide-mouthed jar and cover with 1 cup of water. Drain off the water. Put a swatch of cheesecloth or netting over the mouth of the jar and rinse the seeds twice a day until tails are twice as long as seeds. The same process may be used with all other whole, unhulled seeds (sunflower seeds, vegetable seeds, all dried beans). Serve them to your pet raw, chopped, sautéed, oven toasted, or powdered as a supplement.

Sprouts are highly perishable, so if you have more than you or your pet can readily eat, put them in a jar, cover with cold water, close jar lid, refrigerate, and they will keep nicely for the following 4 to 5 days. Or, if you are really overwhelmed with your sprout harvest, blanch briefly, cool, and store them in airtight pouches in the freezer (you sacrifice all the crunchiness in doing so, however).

SALT AND SALT SUBSTITUTES It is best to keep salt at a minimum in your pet's diet. He is undoubtedly getting more than enough from the prepared foods you feed him. For that reason, salt is left out of most of the recipes here unless it is necessary for some chemical transformation, and then sea salt is used. Kelp (powdered seaweed) is a good substitute. Other salt substitutes include natural soy sauce (tamari) and other natural substances found in health food stores that are aged and do not contain sugar, coloring, or other chemical additives. Miso, a soybean paste aged by fermentation, is also a highly recommended substitute not only for salt but for butter as well (see Mutt Medic #1 for particulars). Usually sold in polyethylene bags, miso looks like dark fruit butter but has a highly concentrated salty, buttery flavor. Often the addition of a few tablespoons of Pet Greens Power Powder (see index) adds sufficient saltiness to any recipe without contributing any sodium.

CAROB POWDER A cocoa and chocolate substitute. Not as sweet, and free of caffein and sugar. Rich in calcium and phosphorus. The carob pods, often sold in health food stores, make good mock dog bones.

BONE MEAL Meat and all-meat dog foods are low in calcium (gross calcium deficiency is manifested by large dogs with dropping rear leg joints or hocks). Meat contains more phosphorus than calcium. Bone meal contains more calcium than phosphorus. Under natural conditions carnivores take great care to balance the calcium deficiency of meat by consuming bones. Two grams of fresh bone supply 380 milligrams of calcium and 190 milligrams of phosphorus. A heavy meat diet should be well supplemented with bone meal. It also delivers goodly amounts of important trace minerals. It is available in large sacks at feed stores and can also be made at home—from bones or, for vegetarian pets, from eggshells (see index).

FATS Fat is necessary as a concentrated source of energy, as a vehicle for carrying fat-soluble vitamins. A diet high in dry kibble will be low in fat. Use bacon drippings (but easy on these—they are salty and not easy to digest), beef tallow, suet, butter, or vegetable shortenings. Other possibilities are homemade butters (see index) and combinations of oils and animal fats. Animals need saturated fats. Cod or halibut fish oils are especially good, since they provide vitamins A and D. And if you or your pet has liver trouble or a tendency in that direction, you can substitute nut butters like sesame butter (just use twice the quantity when substituting).

LIVER POWDER, BREWER'S YEAST Both wonder foods, indeed. Liver powder is a good source of high quality protein as well as the B vitamins, iron, and vitamin A. Yeast (also sold as food or nutritional yeast—do not confuse with baking yeast) is especially important for cats whose protein and vitamin B requirements are higher than those of dogs. Yeast furnishes every B vitamin and essential amino acid in the natural nonsynthetic form for nerve health, muscle function, and prevention of anemia. A good "pepper-upper" for older pets and an important supplement for vegetarian animals.

MILK Not a natural food for weaned dogs and cats. Taken in excess it causes upsets. A bowl of milk a day can supply all of the calories a cat needs but little of the other vitamins and minerals necessary for health and growth. Use the beverages listed under Cat Nips and Dog Dips instead, or where milk protein is desired, substitute yogurt, buttermilk, clabbered milks, nut milk, or soy milk. These products contain low or no amounts of lactose (milk sugar), which may upset the stomach. Pet veterinarians say milk, cow's milk if you do use it, should make up no more than 20 percent of a dog's diet. (Note: All clabbered—sour—milks make superior dog biscuits).

HONEY Dogs have been known to live on nothing but honey and water. It is not a normal dietary item, but lions like it and so does the bear. It is a great natural energizer and, since it is predigested by the bees, is rapidly absorbed by the blood stream. (Refined honey is no better than sugar, since heat alone destroys 50 percent of the healthful properties of the sweetener.) Sick dogs and well puppies benefit by small amounts of first quality, unfiltered, unrefined, unheated organic honey. As for cats, some like it, some do not. For sugar sweetening in a dry form use date sugar or maple sugar.

EGGS Eggs are a natural food for dogs, and they will often lunch upon the eggs of game and sea birds. Dogs can even eat the calcium-rich shell without much processing on your part. Eggs should be cooked because raw egg white destroys the essential B-vitamin biotin. Eggs are a perfect seed-food like nuts, but also like nuts they are rich. No more than five eggs a week or an egg every other day is a generally accepted rule.

SEAWEED *(kelp powder)* There are several types of dried seaweed usually sold in bags in natural food shops and health food stores, as well as some oriental specialty shops. For soup making, kombu and hijicki (a super-smelly, gelantinous sea-spaghetti) are especially appropriate, since they require longer periods of cooking. For quick use, dulse and nori need only toasting. The easiest form in which to use seaweed is perhaps kelp powder, now sold in small shakers. Seaweed can substitute for salt as well as pepper. It is without equal as a source of natural iodine and many other minerals.

SOYBEANS Soybeans, the basis of the basic mock meats, Doggerel I and Doggerel II, are extremely versatile.

They can be turned into cheese, imitation meats, milk, and such high protein seasonings as miso and soy sauce. Supplying complete, low-cost protein, the soybean supplies more vitamin B, and calcium than hamburger. In its liquid form it is more digestible than cow's milk and has twice the iron of beef protein.

FRUITS Dogs generally enjoy all kinds of dried fruits, especially raisins, dates, and figs, as well as raw fruits. They are a fine source of unrefined carbohydrate. Cats are rarely fruit eaters, but there are exceptions. Both cats and dogs seem to enjoy lemon juice and an occasional bowl of applesauce.

(See the appendix, Sources for Mail-Order Supplies, where to buy all the ingredients mentioned if not readily available at your local health food store.)

Boning Up:

Ingredient Recipes

BASIC POWER POWDERS

The following do-it-yourself powders are designed to fortify the nutritional content of commercially prepared pet foods. They are combinations of vitamin-packed ingredients such as raw bone meal, ground dried fish, vegetables, rice, and other grains. Use them liberally on top of, inside of, or along with anything that comes out of a can, pouch, or package. Good for coating foods to be cooked and good as bases for gravies and other good lap-up goos. Store in a cool pantry or refrigerate. You may freeze any surplus.

Pet Greens Power Powder

DRIED CHIVES   1 tablespoon
DRIED PARSLEY   1 tablespoon
DRIED CELERY LEAVES   1 tablespoon
DRIED ONION FLAKES   1 tablespoon
DRIED DILL   1 tablespoon
DRIED SPINACH or DRIED
    LETTUCE (optional)*   1 tablespoon

Combine all ingredients. Use in recipes as directed.

*See Sources for Mail-Order Supplies.

Fish Power Powder

DRIED FISH (WHOLE SHRIMP, MACKEREL,
   HERRING, COD, or MIXTURE)*   ½ pound
KELP POWDER   1 tablespoon

Grind fish, bones and all. Add kelp for a fine fish powder. A good source of natural bone meal and iodine. (If unobtainable, buy ready-to-use codfish flakes at the supermarket.)

*See Sources for Mail-Order Supplies.

Bone Meal Powder *(Homemade)*

EGGSHELLS   1 sackful, washed and dried

Dry eggshells well. Put into blender and grind into fine powder. Store in jars with tight-fitting lids. May be frozen, too. A calcium supplement for vegetarian pets.

Meat Power Powder

RAW BONE MEAL   1 cup
DESICCATED LIVER POWDER and/or
   GLANDULAR ORGAN POWDER*   1 cup
KELP POWDER   ¼ cup

Stir together bone meal, liver powder, and kelp. For meat-eating pets.

* See Sources for Mail-Order Supplies

Sprout Power Powder

SPROUTED GRAINS (RYE, WHEAT,
   BARLEY, OATS, ETC.)   1½ cups

Spread grains on cookie sheet. Bake in 150° oven for 2
hours, stirring and turning twice. Put into mortar and
pound to powder, or pulverize in blender or seed mill to
fine, pasty brown powder.

Meat-Free Power Powder

SOY FLOUR   1 cup
BONE MEAL POWDER
   (HOMEMADE)   as desired (see index)
BREWER'S YEAST   1 cup

Lightly toast flour and combine with other ingredients.
For vegetarian cats and dogs.

Power Powder Paste

SPROUTED SEEDS   1 cup, freshly ground
SPROUTED GRAINS   1 cup, freshly ground
DRY TOAST   1 slice

Put seeds, grains, and toast through meat grinder or
food chopper. Retains all nutrients of fresh sprouts in a
form convenient for supplementing wet pet foods.

Rice Power Powder

NATURAL BROWN RICE   2 cups

Wash and drain rice. Toast lightly in dry skillet, stirring occasionally until golden brown or kernels start popping. Use high heat until rice is dry, then lower to medium. Grind rice in blender to make a powder. Put rice back into skillet and toast lightly again over low heat, stirring until meal gives off nice nutty smells. Store in refrigerator. Good for thickening gravies or for combining with water to make homemade cream of rice porridge.

Power Powder Plus

BONE MEAL POWDER*   1 cup
PET GREENS POWER POWDER*   1 cup
WHEAT GERM or BRAN   1 cup
SPROUT POWDER or FISH POWER
   POWDER*   1 cup
MEAT-FREE POWER POWDER*   1 cup
KELP POWDER   ¼ cup

Stir to combine all ingredients. Refrigerate.

*See index for recipes.

Power Powder Buttons
Cat and Dog Yummies for Prefab Feeding

**BREWER'S YEAST TABLETS
DESICCATED LIVER TABLETS
KELP TABLETS
YOGURT TABLETS
GARLIC TABLETS
COMFREY TABLETS
ALFALFA TABLETS
MALTED MILK TABLETS**

Available at your health food store. But use sparingly—
they are nutrient-rich.

NOTE: To facilitate feeding, you may tuck the tablet
inside a pinch of raw meat or meat substitute.

16 ·

Mutt Butter I

For Meat-eating Pets

FAT (BEEF, PORK, LAMB, or FOWL)   as desired
WATER   as needed

To render fat, cut fat from meat into small chucks; place in heavy saucepan with enough cold water to cover. Bring to a boil and continue to boil until all water is evaporated, remaining liquid is clear, and pieces of fat have browned lightly and shriveled. Stir frequently. When cool, strain and pour into jar.

Mutt Butter II

For Vegetarian Pets

> RAW SESAME SEEDS   1 cup
> NUT OIL   1 tablespoon
> VEGETABLE SEASONING   as desired

Grind sesame seeds repeatedly (seed mill is ideal for this or use blender) until very fine and smooth. Add nut oil and vegetable seasoning. Store. Use twice as much Mutt Butter II in substituting for butter or shortening. Seed butter is digested and assimilated more quickly than animal fats. Fine for pets on low-fat diets, too.

Mutt Butter III

> SOY FLOUR   ¾ cup, lightly toasted
> WATER   ¾ cup
> SEA SALT   1 teaspoon
> VEGETABLE OIL   1 cup

Combine flour with water and salt. Cook in double boiler for 30 minutes. Using wire whisk, whip in oil by hand until thick and creamy. Refrigerate. Another unsaturated-fat margarine.

Mutt Butter IV
Homemade Half-and-Half* Butter

> BEEF TALLOW, LARD, or OTHER
>   SHORTENING   1 cup
> UNSATURATED, UNREFINED "CRUDE" VEGETABLE
>   OIL or NUT OIL   1 cup

Melt down beef tallow as directed for Mutt Butter I; cool slightly and combine with oil. Refrigerate until hardened.

*Half-saturated, half not.

Mutt Butter V

> FRESH COCONUT   1

Use coconut at room temperature. Punch holes in coconut to extract juice. Break nut open and remove white meat. Shave off brown skin with potato peeler; cut meat into small pieces and put through juice extractor. Resulting thick cream will turn into butter under refrigeration.

Mutt Butter VI

> PREPARED SOYBEAN PASTE (MISO)   1 cup
> MUTT BUTTER I, II, III, or IV, or
>   UNREFINED VEGETABLE OIL   1 cup

Buy prepared soybean paste. Blend with any of these mutt butters or with any good unrefined vegetable oil to cut down on saltiness of bean paste. Refrigerate.

Doggerel I

Basic Mock Meat

```
GLUTEN FLOUR*    9 cups
WATER    3 cups, lukewarm
WHOLE-WHEAT FLOUR or GLUTEN FLOUR    ½ cup
```

Measure gluten flour into large mixing bowl. Add water and stir vigorously for 10 minutes to develop the "gluten." Put additional ½ cup gluten or whole-wheat flour on breadboard or counter and knead dough for 20 minutes. When well developed, gluten should be smooth, without any creases, and offer some resistance when you try to push. Put gluten back into bowl and cover with cold water. After 2 hours, pour off water. Put dough ball in colander and knead under running water for about 5 minutes, squeezing out milky, starchy water. Repeat this process at 1-hour intervals until water runs almost clear. This is *raw* gluten. Cut doggerel into chunks, slice into steaks, or grind into "ground meat." You can do just about anything with doggerel that you can do with real meat. Makes 10 or more generous servings.

*Gluten flour is a low-carbohydrate, low-starch, high-protein flour carried by health food stores.

Doggerel II

Another Basic Mock Meat

```
SOY FLOUR      2 cups
WATER      as needed
WATER      1 quart, boiling
APPLE CIDER VINEGAR or
    LEMON JUICE      ½ cup
```

Combine soy flour with ¼ cup cold water, gradually adding more water to make a thick paste. Pour boiling water over mixture.

Put into deep saucepan and set over low heat or in double boiler over hotter surface heat. Bring to a boil and simmer 5 minutes, stirring with whisk. Remove from heat; add vinegar. Strain through fine sieve or cheesecloth after 5 minutes. Save whey for other uses. Chill cheese until solidified. Use 1 heaping tablespoon (or more) to a cup of regular ration as fortification or serve as a meal in itself seasoned with onion, garlic, and finely chopped raw vegetables.

See Bowser By-product #2.

Soy Milk

A No-Lactose, High-Calcium Mutt Milk

DATES   8, pitted
SESAME SEEDS   3 tablespoons
SOY FLOUR or MILK POWDER   about 1½ cups
WATER   enough to make 1 quart

Chop dates. Grind or finely crush sesame seeds. Mix these with soy flour. Put into blender and purée, gradually adding about 4 cups water. Liquefy and store as you would cow's milk. Use up within the week.

NOTE: More dates will make milk thicker, and more liquid will make it thinner.

Fresh Pet Greens

SCALLION GREENS   ½ cup
CHIVES   ½ cup
SPINACH LEAVES   ½ cup
CHARD LEAVES   ½ cup
LETTUCE LEAVES   ½ cup
BROCCOLI LEAVES   ½ cup
PARSLEY   ½ cup
WATERCRESS   ½ cup
RADISH GREENS   ½ cup
DANDELION GREENS   ½ cup
CELERY LEAVES   ½ cup
ALFALFA SPROUTS   ½ cup

Chop and combine all these greens and whatever others may be fresh and in season. Divide into small, airtight, plastic pouches and refrigerate. What you can't use in a week, freeze.

Pet Grass

WHOLE WHEAT, WHOLE RYE, WHOLE BUCKWHEAT
 KERNELS
DIRT or GOOD PLANTING SOIL

Take large planter (the size of a jelly roll pan) with good
drainage and fill ⅔ full of dirt. Mark rows with end of
pencil, leaving ½ inch between rows, and sprinkle in
seeds in fairly close proximity. Cover with dirt, water
generously, and cover tightly with plastic until seeds
begin to sprout. Remove cover and put your planter in
sunlight until grass comes up. If planted in rich soil, this
special "lawn," like sprouted seeds, is rich in natural
vitamins, minerals, enzymes, and trace minerals plus
chlorophyll, which is hard for your pet to come by during winter months. Clip grass with scissors and put
clippings into your pet's rations, or set the whole mini-
lawn down for Tabby to "mow" herself. Meanwhile, start
another plot of Pet Grass.

Grow a mini-lawn for your pet to graze on year-round.

Hound Burger Helper I*

Homemade Bran Flakes

WHOLE GRAIN (WHEAT, CORN, RICE,
   BUCKWHEAT)   2 cups

Take grain that has not been degerminated, hulled, or otherwise processed. Grind twice in corn grinder, coffee mill, seed grinder, or blender. Sift ground grain. (Save what passes through for pastry flour, grinding and sifting it again for finer texture.) Use what remains in sifter as bran flakes to fortify and stretch store-bought pet foods. A good source of fiber for dieter and non-dieter alike.

*See Bowser By-product #4.

Hound Burger Helper II

Homemade Soy Protein

WHOLE DRIED SOYBEANS   4 cups
WATER   8 cups

Soak soybeans in water for 5 hours or overnight. Then put water and beans into blender, 1 cup at a time, and purée. Pour pulp into triple thickness of cheesecloth. Draw up corners and squeeze until "milk" is drawn off. With bean pulp still in cheesecloth, place under cold running water and rinse. Squeeze dry again. Spread out bean pulp, towel-dry, and transfer to ungreased baking sheet. Oven-parch at 350° for 5 to 10 minutes, stirring once or twice. This final step makes pulp light and fluffy. Use to replace part of your cat's or dog's regular ration, to replace a portion of the meat in any meat-based dog food loaf, or to fortify any pet food gravy.

Go To the Boneyard:

Pet Food Recipes

DOG DIPS AND CAT NIPS (DRINKS)

WETTING YOUR PET'S WHISTLE Fluids are an essential part of the balanced animal-diet. Water is especially vital to all-around good health. A dog's water should be of the same quality as yours. It should be changed twice daily but removed during mealtimes to prevent the washing down of a just-eaten meal in a semidigested state, causing indigestion or bloating. A dog can exist on just water for days or even weeks and when sick should be allowed to do so. (Check with your veterinarian, of course, to determine the reason for his illness.)

DOG DIPS For variety and flavor, here are some nourishing and refreshing lap-ups.

Bone Meal Broth I

EGG SHELLS   1 sack, fresh and clean
DISTILLED or SPRING WATER   2 quarts
LEMON JUICE   1 teaspoon
TABLE SCRAPS

Crush eggshells, cover with water, and simmer slowly for 15 minutes. Add lemon juice (to extract minerals from shells) and simmer 15 minutes more. You may add other high-calcium table scraps to fortify it further (parsley, soured raw milk, etc.). Strain and refrigerate.

Bone Meal Broth II

CHICKEN BONES   4 cups, including innards and
   neck bones
EGGSHELLS   ¼ cup, powdered (see Bone Meal
   Powder)
WATER   2 quarts
LEMON JUICE   1 teaspoon

Put chicken bones into pan along with powdered
eggshells. Cover with 2 quarts of water; add lemon
juice. Boil for 10 minutes; then reduce heat and simmer
for 1 hour. Strain and refrigerate. A "toner-upper" in
bone conditions. Supplies necessary organic calcium.

Bran or Oat Broth

WATER   1 quart, hot
ROLLED OATS or COARSE BRAN FLAKES   1 cup
KELP POWDER   to season

Pour water over oats. Let stand overnight, then strain by
pressing in sieve. Reheat until just tepid. Season with
kelp powder, a pinch of wheat germ, or any power
powder.

Lettuce Juice

LETTUCE GREENS   1 sackful
CHIVES or CELERY   handful
WATER   1 tablespoon

How does your pet like greens? Try juicing them. Put shredded lettuce leaves in blender with handful of fresh chives; add water. This instant liquid-salad is both refreshing and nourishing.

Seed Broth
Especially for Dogs

LINSEEDS   1 cup, lightly toasted
RICH VEGETABLE BROTH or BOUILLON   2 cups
SMALL ONION   ½, chopped
EGG YOLKS   2
THICK YOGURT   ½ cup, drained
PET GREENS POWER POWDER or
    PET GRASS   2 tablespoons (see index)

Grind linseeds to a powder. Meanwhile, bring broth to a boil with onion. Simmer gently for 10 minutes, then transfer to double boiler. Gradually stir in the linseed with whisk. Remove from heat. In separate bowl beat eggs with yogurt and greens; stir into thickened soup. Thin soup out with extra broth. Very rich and nutritious. Use parsimoniously to supplement regular pet rations.

Miso Broth

MISO (SOYBEAN PASTE)   1 tablespoon
WATER   1½ cups, warm

Blend miso with water. Mix well; heat until lukewarm. A rejuvenator for well and not-so-well dogs. Cats, too.

Pooch Hootch

Reconstitute any power powder by adding broth or juice and liquefying.

For other dog whistle wetters, see The Gravy Bowl.

CAT NIPS Cats need fluids, too, but tend to consume less water than they should. This tendency is reinforced when cats eat mainly foods that are low in water content. Like dogs, cats should be provided with good, fresh water at all times. For between meals or with food, here are some tasty variations.

Carrot Juice

CARROTS   1 bunch
FRESH PET GREENS or
  PET GRASS   1 tablespoon (see index)

With juice extractor make carrot juice fresh from raw
carrots. Add pet greens. (No extractor? Cook the carrots until soft and liquefy along with the cooking juices in
your blender.) A wonderful sauce for meatless meals,
for moistening dry kibble, for packing vitamin A into
puss's diet.

Fish Nip
Broth for Piscine Puss

FISH BONES   as many as you can muster
WATER   as directed
CELERY LEAVES and ONION
  SCRAPS   a heap
STOCKPOT VEGETABLES
SEAWEED   1 leaf
CARROT   1 or 2, chopped

Put all your stockpiled fish bones into pot and cover with
water. Add remaining ingredients. Boil, then lower heat
and simmer covered for 30 minutes. Strain and refrigerate or freeze in ice cube tray for instant bouillon
cubes. Rich in iodine and phosphorus.

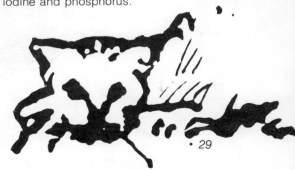

Fish-Not Nip

Seaweed Broth for Vegetarian Tabbies

```
GARLIC CLOVE     1
MEDIUM ONION     ½, sliced and chopped
COLD PRESSED VEGETABLE OIL    2 tablespoons
DRIED SEAWEED (Hijicki)*    1 cup, unsalted
LENTIL SPROUTS    ½ cup
HOMEMADE VEGETABLE BROTH     3 cups, unsalted
SOY SAUCE     1 teaspoon
MISO    1 tablespoon
SEA SALT     1 teaspoon
WATERCRESS, PARSLEY, or CHIVES
    (optional) chopped
```

Chop garlic or put through a press; add garlic and onion to heated oil in deep pot. Sauté for 2 to 5 minutes. Add seaweed, torn into pieces, and lentil sprouts with 2 cups broth and soy sauce. Turn heat down and simmer for 15 minutes. Blend miso into last cup broth and add miso mixture, sea salt, and watercress to pot. Heat until lukewarm.

This fishy, salty broth contains neither fish nor salt. Miso should have a smooth, yet stimulating, unctuous quality. It is good for the intestinal flora and is high in protein of a type that is easily assimilated.

*See Sources for Mail-Order Supplies.

For other cat whistle wetters, see bone meal broths and soy milk.

BONERS (BONES AND BOGUS BONES)
BONING UP ON BONES Beginning with Old Mother Hubbard's poor doggie, the dog who gets "none" is indeed unhappy and possibly unhealthy. But we must be careful about the bones we feed our pets. The small bones in breast of lamb and veal are readily digestible by dogs in good health. For the family cat, leg bones from beef or lamb may be served or big knuckle bones cut into sections. Avoid bones that can splinter, like chop and chicken bones. Vegetarian dog bones for the noncarnivorous canine include corncobs, lightly roasted cabbage stumps or raw roots such as turnip for safe, splinter-proof gnawing. For sweet-tooth teething and high-mineral chewing try dark, pungent-smelling carob pods, sold at health food stores, or squares of honeycomb. Or manufacture your own:

Fake Gristle

DRIED KOMBU (SEAWEED)*   6-inch lengths
ANY TASTY BROTH

Bake kombu in moderate oven for 10 minutes, dip, and soak a few minutes in broth. Serve crispy and crunchy. For the vegetarian dog that wants to chew the fat.

*Available at your health food store.

THE GRAVY BOWL

The following gravies, sauces, broths, and miscellaneous "pour-ons" have been designed as nutritious wetting solutions for both homemade and store-bought pet food rations. Most are good with any dry, semimoist, or canned foods and can even double as soups on cold days.

Gravy I

BREWER'S YEAST FLAKES or POWDER   ½ cup
FLOUR   ¼ cup
OIL or FAT   ⅓ cup
WATER   as needed
SOY SAUCE   2 to 3 tablespoons
KELP POWDER   ½ teaspoon

Combine yeast and flour and roast in dry pan until it gives off toasted aroma. Add oil and stir while mixture bubbles and turns golden. Add water, still stirring until it changes to consistency of gravy. Stir in soy sauce and kelp. A cheese-flavored sauce rich in vitamin B.

Gravy II

BREWER'S YEAST FLAKES or
   POWDER   1 cup
FLOUR $1/3$ cup
CORNSTARCH or ARROWROOT
   POWDER   3 tablespoons
SEA SALT   1½ teaspoons
KELP POWDER   1½ teaspoons
WATER   2 cups
FAT   ½ cup, melted
WET MUSTARD   2 teaspoons

Combine dry ingredients in saucepan. Gradually add water, making a smooth paste, and then thin with remaining water. Place over burner and heat, stirring constantly until mixture thickens and bubbles. Let mixture bubble 1 minute; then remove from heat and beat in fat and mustard.* Use either as a supernutritional sauce to soup up any out-of-the-can supper, as a fortification mixed half-and-half with commercial rations, or as a soup supper if your collie is a soup-hound at heart.

*For another yeast treat see Bowser By-product #3.

Gravy III

Gravy Grains

WHOLE GRAINS (WHEAT, RICE,
  OATS, BARLEY)   2 cups
WATER   as needed

Spread grains over ungreased cookie sheet. Roast in 350° oven for about 35 to 45 minutes or until browned, but not burned—stirring every 10 minutes. Pour browned grains (warm or cooled) into any grinding gadget and grind into a fine powder. Store in dark-tinted jars in dark, cool place. To use, boil or percolate approximately 2 tablespoons for every 6 ounces of water. Do not overboil. Cool and serve as a broth or thicken by blending 1 or 2 tablespoons of any power powder (see index) or 1 or 2 tablespoons of miso for meaty, flavorful gravy. Serve lukewarm or cool over dry kibble, semimoist chunks, or canned food.

See Bowser By-product #8 for leftover uses.

Gravy IV

Sesame Sauce

CANNED OR HOMEMADE TAHINI*   ⅓ cup
WATER   ⅓ cup, cold
GARLIC CLOVE   ½ teaspoon chopped
SALT   1 teaspoon
LEMON JUICE   ½ cup

Spoon tahini into bowl; add water, a tablespoon at a time. Crush garlic and salt to a smooth paste using blade of knife; add to blender along with tahini. Purée at low speed, gradually adding lemon juice. Gravy will turn pale and thin. Refrigerate. For boosting your pet's calcium intake.

*Tahini is a paste made from ground sesame seeds.

Gravy V

OIL   1 tablespoon
ONION or FRESH PET GREENS   ½ cup (see index)
TAHINI (SESAME PASTE)   ½ cup
WATER   4 tablespoons
MISO   2 tablespoons

Warm oil in 1½-quart pan. Stir in onion, cover, and cook over medium heat for 2 minutes. Remove lid from pan and let onions brown slowly, 3 to 4 minutes. Add tahini and stir over medium heat for 3 to 5 minutes. When mixture is milky coffee color, stir in water, a tablespoon at a time. Then add miso, a tablespoon at a time. Stir over heat for 2 more minutes. Makes 1 cup muzzle-lickin' good gravy.

MAIN DISHES

These main dish recipes include, for the most part, mock meats—grain or grain/bean combinations designed to give your pet high-quality vegetarian protein.

Mutt's Applesauce*

Uncooked and Unsweetened

LARGE RIPE APPLES	2, unpeeled and unsprayed
UNSWEETENED CIDER	1 cup
LEMON JUICE	½ teaspoon
POWDERED WHEY	¼ cup
YOGURT, SOUR CREAM, or PLAIN	
ICE CREAM	1 tablespoon
KELP POWDER	pinch

Chop apples, discarding core and stem. Put into blender with cider; purée. Add remaining ingredients and blend on low until well mixed. Refrigerate. Use up in 10 days.

Apples—even if they don't completely ward off the dog doctor—aid a dog's digestion and the pectin therein is a powerful force for good in pet as in man. Since a large share of the nutrients occur in the peel, don't pare it away (peelings also help give homemade sauce a rosier hue). Perfect for dieting dogs and a good puppy-stuffer!

*See Bowser By-product #11.

Big Burger Bits

WATER   4 cups
SEA SALT   2 teaspoons
STONE-GROUND WHOLE YELLOW
    CORNMEAL   2 cups (10 ounces)
ANY PET POWDERS   ¼ cup or
    PET GRASS   2 teaspoons

Bring water to a boil in heavy 2-quart pot or heavy iron skillet. Add salt to water; then slowly whisk in remaining ingredients. Cook over low heat, tightly covered, for 20 minutes. For crusty "bits" cook uncovered over low heat for 20 more minutes until meal pulls away from sides of pot and a crusty bottom and outer edge form. Chill until well solidified. Cut into square "burger bits" and sauté in any mutt butter or serve warm with something from The Gravy Bowl.

Bowser's Dried Beef

FLANK STEAK   2½ pounds
SOY SAUCE   ½ cup
GARLIC SALT   ¼ teaspoon
BLACK PEPPER   to season, ground

Trim all visible fat from steak (jerky keeps indefinitely if you do). Slice steak lengthwise with the grain in long, thin slices. Combine soy sauce, garlic, and pepper. Pour over beef strips and marinate for 1 hour. Place strips on wire rack over baking sheet. Arrange strips so they do not overlap. Bake at 150° to 175° for 10 to 12 hours. Store in airtight canister.

Cat's Cold Cuts

CHICKEN BROTH   1 cup
UNFLAVORED GELATIN   4 envelopes
TUNA FISH   2 7-ounce cans, drained
PLAIN YOGURT   16 ounces
LEMON JUICE   2 tablespoons
ANCHOVY FILLETS   2 tablespoons, drained

Put broth into small pan. Stir in gelatin and let soak 2 to 3 minutes. Place over low heat until dissolved and clear (3 to 4 minutes). Let cool until needed. Put 2 cans of tuna fish, 1 carton of yogurt, lemon juice, and anchovy fillets into blender and blend until smooth. Add dissolved gelatin to mixture and stir. Pour mixture into lightly oiled glass loaf pan and chill until firm, 3 hours or more. Loosen loaf from sides of pan, then turn out onto board or platter. Cut into ¼-inch cold cuts. Makes 24. Let stand before serving to remove the chill.

Shrimp Paste for Free

SHRIMP SHELLS   from 1 pound
    of fresh shrimp, any size
CREAM, WATER, or SOY
    MILK   small amount (see index)
FOOD YEAST or ANY POWER
    POWDER   1 teaspoon (see index)
PARSLEY   1 teaspoon chopped

Rinse shells in warm water and combine with small amount of cream in blender. Process until a smooth purée; add yeast and parsley and mix well. Serve as supplement to any commercial cat food. Or, thin with water and serve as soup.

Canine Cottage Cheese

CHEESE RENNET*   1 tablet
WATER   2 tablespoons
SKIM MILK   1 gallon

Dissolve rennet tablet in water and stir into milk. (If you happen to have some sour milk, use a cup to replace 1 cup of skim.) Warm milk slightly, stirring constantly. Milk should be lukewarm (about 85° to 90°). Set milk aside for 30 minutes to clabber. Cut firmed milk into cubes and put into double boiler. Heat it gradually until temperature reaches about 110°. Hold curd at this temperature for about 30 minutes, stirring often. Pour both curds and whey into colander lined with double thickness of cheesecloth and let whey drain off. Immerse bag in bowl of cold water, then spoon contents into another bowl. Refrigerate and serve straight or as canned food supplement.

*Rennet—made from the enzyme rennin—is a substance used to curdle milk.

Snap, Crackle, Pup

A Fortifying Pooch Porridge

CORNMEAL   8 parts
SOY GRITS or SOY FLOUR   2 parts
CRACKED RYE (RYE MEAL)   5 parts
CRACKED BUCKWHEAT GROATS
   (KASHA)   2 parts
MILLET   1 part
WATER   boiling
SOY MILK or BONE
   MEAL BROTH   as desired (see index)

Combine all dry ingredients with 3 times as much water. Put into saucepan; cook over medium heat, stirring constantly until it starts to thicken. Reduce heat and cook 25 minutes longer. Cool and top with soy milk or bone meal broth. Serve to the family cat or dog. Leftovers can be chilled, sliced, and sautéed.

Siamese Seviche

LIME JUICE or HALF LIME,
   HALF LEMON JUICE   ⅔ cup
GARLIC CLOVE   ½ teaspoon minced
SWEET ONION   8 very thin slices
SEA SALT   ½ teaspoon
BLACK PEPPER   a good grating
SOLE, FLOUNDER, or
   OTHER WHITE FISH   1 pound

Mix all ingredients together except fish. Cut fish into strips about 2 inches long and ¼ inch wide. Cover fish strips with juice mixture. Cover and refrigerate for at

least 3 hours or as long as 24 hours. When ready, the juice has "cooked" the fish and it is quite deliciously safe to eat.

See Bowser By-product #5.

Doggie Dodgers
High-Fiber Dog Biscuits

WHITE or YELLOW CORNMEAL   1½ cups
CORN BRAN or OTHER HOMEMADE
  BRAN FLAKES   ½ cup (see index)
KELP POWDER   ¼ teaspoon
ANY POWER POWDER   2 tablespoons (see index)
CORN OIL   ⅙ cup
WATER   about 3 cups, boiling

Combine all ingredients except water. Pour on boiling water and mix. Let mixture cool and shape into patties. If mixture is too wet, add a little meal or flour until consistency is right. Place biscuits on greased baking sheet and bake at 375° for 10 minutes. Turn with spatula and bake for 10 minutes more. Cool before serving. Can be broken up and served with gravy, too.

For a dietetic version, see Diet Dog Dodgers.

Hot Diggity Dogs

ONION   4 tablespoons minced
GARLIC CLOVE   1, crushed
CRACKED WHEAT   ½ cup
SEED or NUT OIL   2 tablespoons
HOMEMADE BROTH   small amount (see index)
UNSALTED NUTS   ½ cup
WHOLE EGG   1, beaten
MILD CHEESE   ¼ cup, grated
POTATO   ½ cup finely grated
KELP POWDER   to season
ANY POWER POWDER   4 tablespoons (see index)

Sauté onion and garlic in oil. Stir in cracked wheat, coat well with oil, and add small amount of broth. Cover tightly and steam for 10 minutes. Grind nuts into a meal in seed mill or blender; mix with egg. Put in bowl with steamed grain, cheese, potato, seasoning, and pet powder. If mixture is too moist to shape, add more ground nuts or a bit of flour. Shape into "sausages" and bake in greased hollows of corn stick pan, or side by side on greased baking sheet. Bake at 325° for 30 minutes. Serve with Mutt Mustard, what else?

Mutt Mustard

EGG YOLKS   2, at room temperature
SOY OIL   1 cup, at room temperature
LEMON JUICE   2 teaspoons
TURMERIC   pinch
DRY MUSTARD   pinch
KELP POWDER   1 teaspoon

Put yolks into blender; add ¼ cup oil and lemon juice. Blend at medium speed. Removing the insert in blender cap and keeping blender at low speed, gradually add remaining oil. When all oil is absorbed, stop blender motor, add seasonings, and replace insert. Blend at high speed for a few seconds. Mustard will be very yellow, very creamy, and very smooth. Serve with Hot Diggity Dogs.

Swiss-Style Mutt Muesli

DATES   6, pitted
ROLLED OATS   2 cups
WHEAT GERM or BRAN   ¼ cup, raw or toasted
SEEDS or NUTS   4 teaspoons
SWISS HERBS*   1 tablespoon

Put dates into blender, then add 1 cup oats and wheat germ. Whirl until crumbly. Mix with remaining oats, seeds, and herbs in bowl. Serve with lukewarm soy milk (see index).

*Available at health food stores or substitute catnip leaves for cats, slippery elm powder or cherry bark for dogs. These herbs are also sold in tea form at natural food shops.

Mutt Balls

HOUND BURGER HELPER II   1 cup (see index)
WHOLE-WHEAT FLOUR   ½ cup
WHOLE EGG   1, lightly beaten
ONION   ¼ cup, minced
FRESH PET GREENS or PET
   GRASS   ¼ cup (see index)
SOY SAUCE   1 tablespoon
KELP POWDER   dash
OIL or FAT   enough for frying or deep-frying

Combine everything except cooking oil. Mix well. Shape into meatballs with wet hands. Heat oil to 350° in skillet or deep fryer and drop in balls, turning with metal tongs to brown on all sides. Drain and cool. Makes about 10 tasty mutt balls. See The Gravy Bowl for suitable sauce.

Pupcorn Bread

RAISINS   ¼ cup
CORNMEAL   1 cup
SOY FLOUR   ½ cup
KELP POWDER   2 teaspoons
HONEY   1 to 2 tablespoons
NUT BUTTER (ALMOND, PEANUT,
   CASHEW)   ½ cup
SHORTENING   4 tablespoons
WATER   ⅛ cup

Put raisins through food grinder. Mix next 6 ingredients together; add raisins. Then add water and form a loaf. Wrap in wax paper, press into loaf pan or can to shape. Slice as needed—when hunger strikes.

Dog Bites

DOG BISCUITS or PLAIN CRACKERS   1 cup
GRITS (SOY, CORN, BULGUR, CEREAL)   1 cup
SUNFLOWER SEEDS   1 cup
PEANUT BUTTER   2 tablespoons
BEEF SUET   to make 1½ cups melted

Grind up biscuits in blender and put into mixing bowl. Add grits, then seeds and peanut butter. Put suet through meat grinder, then melt in top of double boiler. Remove from heat; let cool and harden slightly. Reheat and pour 1½ cups over biscuit mixture; mix well. Press into casserole dish and, when well set, cut into bite-sized squares. A super snack fortified with natural fat.

If your pet must have three squares a day, try these!

Kibble I
All-Purpose Dog and Cat Chow

RAW DOGGEREL I   2 cups
HOMEMADE MEAT BROTH   2 cups or
    MISO   2 tablespoons dissolved in 2 cups hot water

Soak doggerel in broth for 2 hours or more. Remove from marinade and cut into big squares; poach in skillet in same broth for 30 minutes. Drain and blot dry. Put doggerel through meat grinder using coarse blade. Kibble will emerge in thick spaghettilike strands. Spread strands over greased cookie sheet so they do not overlap. Bake at 250° until soft but firm for soft, moist kibble, or until brown and crisp for dry kibble. Cool and pack in polyethylene pouches and store in dry, cool place.

Kibble II
Dry-Roasted Dog Chow

WHOLE DRY SOYBEANS   3 cups
WATER   6 cups
SALT   to season
KELP POWDER   to season

Soak beans for 5 to 6 hours in water. Drain well and dry. Transfer beans to large ungreased cookie sheets and spread in thin layer. Place in unheated oven and roast at 200 ° to 250 ° for 2 to 2½ hours or until beans are light brown. Shake pans once every 20 minutes if convenient. While beans are slightly soft, remove from oven, sprinkle lightly with salt and kelp, and set aside to cool slightly. Put beans in blender (½ cup at a time) and chop at low speed for about 30 seconds until chunky and kibbled. Makes 3 cups of meat-free kibble at a cost of about 30 cents. For further fortification serve with any sauce from The Gravy Bowl.

Pupernickel Bread
Raw, Unrefined Refrigerator Loaf

BLACK FIGS   2 cups
ALMONDS, PECANS, or PEANUTS
   (or COMBINATION)   2 cups
WHEAT GERM or BRAN   enough to stiffen
   the mixture

Grind figs and nuts together in meat grinder or food mill; add enough wheat germ to make stiff mixture. Put entire mixture through grinder again—this reprocessing is essential to turning out a well-mixed loaf. Form into long loaf, wrap in wax paper. Put into coffee can and chill; remove and slice thin.

Kibble Plus

Meat-free Dog Meal – Complete Protein

WHOLE DRY SOYBEANS   2 cups
SPROUTED GRAINS (WHEAT, RYE,
    OAT, etc.)   1 cup
CORNMEAL   1 cup

See directions for soaking and roasting soybeans in Kibble II. Half an hour before soybeans are fully roasted, spread cornmeal and sprouted grain over separate baking sheet and put into oven on separate rack. Finish baking. Remove when sprouts are dry and slightly crisp. Put soybeans into blender and blender-chop at low speed for just 30 seconds. Combine grain, ground corn, and chopped beans. Sprinkle with kelp if desired and store in coffee cans or canisters in dry, cool place. Extra kibble may be frozen.

NOTE: The amino acid patterns of soybeans are complemented by those of grains such as corn and sprouted grain, yielding a protein-packed substance which is the equal of most meat products and is free of the chemical additives in commercial dry foods.

Kibble for Cats

SOYBEANS   3 cups
WATER or ANY CAT NIP   6 cups (see index)
KELP POWDER   to season
DRIED SHRIMP or CODFISH
   FLAKES   to season, ground

Soak soybeans in water for 5 to 6 hours or overnight. Drain and dry. Spread beans over greased cookie sheet in single layer. Roast for 2 to 2½ hours at 200° to 250°. Stir at 20- to 30-minute intervals. When beans are still slightly soft, remove and sprinkle with kelp and shrimp (grind to a powder in seed mill or blender). Put into blender and chop on low speed in 1-cup batches until reduced to coarse meal. Serve well moistened with any cat nip, with or without kitty's regular canned or boxed meal. Soybeans contain almost as much usable protein as chicken, so put a cluck in your kibble!

Pooch Pasties
Wheat-free, Single-Ingredient Dog Biscuits

SPROUTED GARBANZO
   BEANS (chickpeas)   2 cups
CORNMEAL (optional)   small amount

Put freshly sprouted beans through meat grinder and shape resulting paste (with or without optional cornmeal) into 3 "ropes." Wet your hands if dough seems sticky. Coil ropes so that you have 3 round, snail-shaped dog biscuits. Put biscuits on lightly greased cookie sheets and bake at 250° for 1 hour. Turn after 30 minutes to brown them evenly.

Doggerolls

Mock Pork Sausage for Mock-Meat Eaters

HOUND BURGER HELPER II   4 cups (see index)
WHOLE-WHEAT FLOUR · · 1 cup
RAW BRAN   1 cup
SHORTENING, RENDERED FAT, or
    VEGETABLE OIL   ¾ cup, melted
SOY MILK or DAIRY MILK   1 cup
BREWER'S YEAST   2 cups
FENNEL SEED   1 teaspoon
BLACK PEPPER   1 teaspoon
SOY SAUCE   ¼ cup
OREGANO   3 teaspoons
KELP POWDER   2 teaspoons
HONEY   1 tablespoon
GARLIC POWDER   2 tablespoons
MUSTARD   2 tablespoons
ALLSPICE   2 teaspoons
PET GREENS POWER
    POWDER   1 tablespoon (see index)
WATER   boiling, for steaming

Mix all ingredients together thoroughly. Divide mixture into 4 parts; spoon each part into a triple thickness of dampened cheesecloth and secure. Put rolls into 4 soup cans with 1 end removed. Set cans on rack over water boiling in deep kettle. Cover and steam for 1 hour, adding water in kettle as needed. Cool sausage 10 minutes in cans. Remove. Chill in refrigerator before slicing and frying—and bestowing upon a friendly, hungry dog.

Mutt Loaf I

MEDIUM CARROTS   3, coarsely chopped
MEDIUM BOILING ONION   1, quartered
PARSLEY or FRESH PET
   GREENS   ½ cup chopped (see index)
RAW OATMEAL   ½ cup
CRACKED WHEAT or BULGUR   ½ cup
WHEAT FLAKES   ½ cup
HOMEMADE VEGETABLE BROTH or BONE
   MEAL BROTH   1 cup (see index)
BONE MEAL POWDER
   (HOMEMADE)   2 tablespoons (see index)
SOY GRANULES or GRITS   ¼ cup
WHOLE EGG   1
CORNMEAL   as needed, fresh-ground

Put carrots, onion, and parsley through food grinder. Soak oatmeal, cracked wheat, and wheat flakes in broth for 15 minutes. Combine soaked grains, ground vegetables, powder, soy granules, and egg in mixing bowl; mix well. If loaf seems a bit "wet," add cornmeal. Put mixture into greased loaf pan lightly dusted with cornmeal and bake at 350° for 30 minutes. When cool, cut into chunks and transfer to a refrigerator container. Makes 12 good-sized meat-extender chunks for canned or semimoist commercial pet foods.

RAW MUTT LOAF: Follow the general directions but add ½ cup more liquid and soak 1 hour. Omit baking. Use as you would ground meat to supplement semimoist or canned dog food.

Mutt Loaf II
Meat-free, Wheat-free

SOY FLOUR   2 cups or
   SOY FLOUR and SOY GRANULES   1 cup, each
CORNSTARCH or ARROWROOT STARCH   1½ cups
BUTTER or MUTT BUTTER   3 tablespoons
   (see index)
MISO   1 tablespoon
FRESH PET GREENS or PET GREENS
   POWER POWDER   ½ cup (see index)
HOMEMADE BROTH   1½ cups, hot (see index)

Combine all ingredients except broth and mix well.
Pour on boiling broth and mix to combine completely.
Spoon into lightly greased loaf pan and bake at 350° for
1 hour. Cool and cut into slices or squares. Refrigerate
unused portions. Good as a snack, under gravy, and as
a meat-stretcher.

Hush Puppies

WHOLE EGGS   2
DATES   1 cup, pitted and blended smooth
CAROB POWDER   2 tablespoons
BONE MEAL POWDER
   (HOMEMADE)   1 cup (see index)
VEGETABLE SHORTENING   ½ cup

Purée eggs and dates. Pour into bowl and gradually
add dry ingredients and shortening. Bake at 325° for 25
minutes. When cooled, cut into squares. This concoc-
tion is quite palatable for people, too. For a dogs-only
version, substitute ½ cup grated and squeezed turnip
plus ½ cup well-cooked, drained peas for the dates.

Rollovers

Green-Pea Turnovers for Towser

WHOLE-WHEAT FLOUR   2 cups
KELP POWDER   ½ teaspoon
BAKING POWDER   1 teaspoon
ANY POWER POWDER or HOMEMADE
  BRAN FLAKES   ½ cup (see index)
WHOLE EGGS   2
VEGETABLE OIL   ½ cup
WATER   2 tablespoons

In large mixing bowl sift together flour, kelp, and baking powder. Stir in power powder. Beat eggs in separate bowl. Toss flour mixture lightly and add eggs gradually. Add oil drop by drop, stirring briskly to make a crumbly mixture. Gradually add enough cold water to make a soft dough. Chill dough before rolling. Heat oven to 400°; grease 2 baking sheets. On floured board roll dough into ¼-inch-thick rectangle. Trim ragged edges with knife and cut dough into 24 squares of about 3 x 3 inches. Spoon about ¼ cup filling (see below) on each of 12 squares. Moisten edges of filled squares lightly with water and top each with unfilled square. Pinch 4 edges with fork or fingers to seal. Put rollovers on baking sheet and brush surfaces with oil. Bake rollovers at 325° until golden brown (about 35 minutes). A meal in itself, a meal between meals, a premeal warm-up. Refrigerate or freeze any extras.

Filling for Rollovers

WATER 2½ cups
UNCOOKED SPLIT PEAS 1 cup
LARGE ONION 1, diced
OIL ⅓ cup
WHOLE EGGS 2
KELP POWDER 1 teaspoon

In water, cook peas over low heat in covered saucepan for about 1 hour. Let stand until peas are just warm. Dice onion. Mash peas and combine with onion, oil, eggs, and kelp.

Mealies
Between Meals or a Meal in Itself

MILLET ½ cup
WATER or HOMEMADE
  BROTH 1½ cups (see index)
FRUIT 2 tablespoons chopped
NUTS 2 tablespoons chopped or ground
SALT or KELP POWDER to season
SHORTENING 1 tablespoon

Soak millet overnight. Next day combine it with water and bring to a boil. Reduce heat; simmer until all liquid is absorbed. Stir in remaining ingredients except shortening. Melt shortening in heavy-bottomed skillet; form millet mixture into pancake shapes and cook until golden on each side. To "rusk" mealies for a later snack, dry them in 200° oven for 2 hours. Cool and store in canister. Mealies will keep for a week. To serve, break up and mix with broth, canned food, or regular ration.

Wheat Balls for Wolfhounds

Mock Meatballs

WHOLE EGGS   2, separated
WHEAT SPROUTS   ½ cup chopped
WHOLE-GRAIN FLOUR   ½ cup
SOY SAUCE   2 tablespoons
SCALLION   1, finely chopped
FRESH PET GREENS or
    PET GRASS   2 tablespoons minced (see index)
WATER   boiling

Beat egg whites until stiff. Combine egg yolks with all other ingredients, folding in beaten whites last. With greased hands, shape mixture into 12 small balls and place in greased steamer. Fill pot with boiling water and insert steamer; cover tightly and steam balls for 15 minutes. Good cold as a between-meal snack or warm with the following gravy.

Wheat Balls Gravy

BONE MEAL POWDER   ¼ cup (see index)
WATER   2 cups
SESAME SEEDS   ¼ cup toasted
ANY MUTT BUTTER   2 tablespoons (see index)
ONION FLAKES   2 teaspoons
ARROWROOT STARCH   2 tablespoons
KELP POWDER   1 teaspoon

Purée all ingredients in blender and transfer to saucepan. Cook over medium heat, stirring until thickened.

Rover's Ribs
Vegetarian Barbecue

DOGGEREL I   2 cups (see index)
BREWER'S YEAST   ⅓ cup
MUTT BUTTER or PEANUT
   BUTTER   ½ cup (see index)
PAPRIKA   2 tablespoons
SEA SALT or KELP POWDER   3 tablespoons
LARGE ONION   1, chopped
FAT   ⅔ cup
VEGETABLE OIL   ¼ cup

Put doggerel into mixing bowl with yeast, mutt butter, paprika, and salt. Sauté onion in fat and pour over doggerel mixture. While still warm, mix well with fingers until all ingredients are combined and gluten is in stringy chunks. Break doggerel up into good-sized, 2 x 4-inch "ribs" and flatten them to ¼-to ½-thickness. Do not roll: rolling will give them doughy rather than chewy texture. Pour oil on cookie sheet, top with "ribs"; bake for 1 hour at 350° until crispy and brown. Turn after 30 minutes to brown evenly if desired. If sauce is in order, pour on and bake an extra 10 minutes at 400°.

Pet Greens Pasta
Vegetable Fettuccine

WHOLE-WHEAT FLOUR   2 cups
WHOLE EGGS or YOLKS   2
LARGE SPINACH LEAVES WITH STEMS   4
FRESH PET GREENS or
   PET GRASS   ¼ cup (see index)
WATER, SOY MILK, or
   BONE MEAL BROTH   as needed (see index)

Warm flour to room temperature. Put eggs in blender; add spinach and greens; purée until smooth. Put flour into large mixing bowl, make a well in the middle, and pour in egg mixture. Blend together using fingers. When well mixed, gradually add water a few drops at a time using just enough to make a kneading consistency. Knead dough for about 5 minutes. Cover and let stand 15 minutes. Flour board and roll out dough to ¼-inch thickness. Sprinkle dough lightly with more flour and, using sharp knife, cut into noodles. Spread noodles out on wax paper or hang over wire hangers on backs of chairs to dry thoroughly. Wrap in foil and refrigerate until needed. To use, simmer in small amount of water. Cool and serve with cooking juices. Makes a delicious vegetable fettuccine for you or your pet.

See Bowser By-product #9.

Mock Chopped Liver for Cats

GREEN BEANS   ¾ to 1 pound
WATER   boiling
OIL   2 tablespoons
ONION   1, finely chopped
LARGE GARLIC CLOVE   1, pressed and minced
WHOLE EGG   1, hard-cooked
KELP POWDER   pinch

Trim beans and cook covered in small amount of water until tender. Heat oil and brown onion and garlic lightly. Drain beans and chop or grind finely. Mash egg with beans, then blend in onions, garlic, and kelp to form compact mass. Chill. Serve as a kitty canapé on little squares of rusk.

Chapati Chapati Chihuahua
A Flatbread for Four-footed Friends

WHOLE-WHEAT FLOUR   1¼ cups
HOUND BURGER HELPER II   ½ cup (see index)
SEA SALT or KELP POWDER   ½ teaspoon
WATER   2 tablespoons
OIL   1 tablespoon

Preheat oven to 350°. Combine 1 cup flour with remaining ingredients. Mix well; then turn out on surface floured with remaining flour and knead for 5 minutes. When dough is smooth, divide into 8 parts and roll each one out into a 6-inch circle. Place circles on baking sheets and bake until nicely browned—5 to 10 minutes. For puffy *chapatis,* deep-fry in 350° oil for 30 seconds. Turn and continue cooking until puffed up. Drain and serve as a dog biscuit snack or as a tasty "twofer" (for pet and pet proprietor).

Grranola

All-Purpose Pet Chow

ROLLED OATS   1 cup
WHOLE-WHEAT FLAKES*   1 cup
RYE, SOY, or RICE FLAKES*   1 cup
SPLIT PEAS or LENTILS   1 cup ground
GARLIC FLAKES   1 tablespoon
ONION FLAKES   1 tablespoon
BREWER'S YEAST   1 or more tablespoons
BONE MEAL POWDER   1 tablespoon
   or more (see index)
OIL or RENDERED FAT   1 cup (see Mutt Butters)

Combine everything in large mixing bowl; mix well. Spread mixture in single layer over greased baking sheet (jelly roll pan is best). Bake at 275° for about 45 minutes stirring occasionally with spatula to brown evenly. Makes 3 cups. Double the order if you have a big dog.

NOTE: You may press the oil of a large clove of garlic over the Grranola after it comes out of the oven or store Grranola for a day with a clove or two of peeled garlic in a tightly closed canister to heighten its palatability—for your dog, if not for yourself!

*See Sources for Mail-Order Supplies.

Pringled Pet Chips

WHITE or YELLOW CORNMEAL   ½ cup
WHOLE-WHEAT FLOUR   ½ cup
GARLIC SALT or ONION SALT   ½ teaspoon
HOMEMADE MEAT or VEGETABLE
    BROTH   ¼ cup (see index)

Combine dry ingredients and gradually add broth until a nonsticky but soft dough is formed. Knead dough briefly and let rest under damp towel for 1 hour. Heat heavy skillet and when medium-hot, dust with additional cornmeal. Tear off small balls of dough and roll very thin. Cut out circles with coffee can lid. Bake in skillet until dry. Turn and bake on opposite side. Do not overbake. "Pringle" the chips by folding carefully and placing inside an empty napkin holder to shape—about 1 minute to "set." Remove and repeat with remaining dough. Stack chips one inside the other and store in large coffee can or canister with tight-fitting snap-on lid. May also be frozen. Makes about 1 dozen 6-inch chips. A treat to eat that provides plenty of unrefined natural carbohydrate. Good enough for owner to share with pet!

Woofles

A Wonder Waffle for Wonder Dogs

FLOUR (RICE, CORN, RYE, or a MIXTURE)   1 cup
SEA SALT or KELP POWDER   ½ teaspoon
BAKING SODA   1 teaspoon
WHOLE EGGS   2
HONEY   2 tablespoons
BUTTERMILK or YOGURT   ¾ cup
ANY MUTT BUTTER   ¼ cup (see index)
SPROUT POWER POWDER   ¾ cup (see index)

Sift flour, salt, and baking soda into large mixing bowl. In small bowl, beat eggs until frothy, add honey; combine with flour mixture. Add milk, mutt butter, and sprout powder. Lightly grease and preheat waffle iron; pour on batter. Bake until crisp. Serve out of the hand or broken in bits and moistened with an appropriate cat nip or dog dip. Store in refrigerator or in airtight cookie canister.

Pooched Eggs

An Egg-free, Two-Ingredient Breakfast

DOGGEREL II   1 cup (see index)
YOGURT   2 tablespoons
ANY MUTT BUTTER   about 1 tablespoon (see index)
ANY POWER POWDER   sprinkle (see index)

Beat Doggerel II with yogurt; melt butter in skillet and scramble mixture. Sprinkle with any power powder. Serves 1 pooch or 2 puppies.

Fidol

Freezer-dried Meat-free Pet Food

DOGGEREL II   1 batch (see index)
HOMEMADE BROTH (MEAT-BASED or
  NON-MEAT-BASED)   (see index)
WATER   boiling
WATER   cold or lukewarm

When Doggerel II cools, cut into cubes and marinate in broth for 2 hours or more. Drain and place cubes (leaving 1 inch or more space between) on large platter. Freeze at very low temperature for 3 days for porous and resilient texture; freeze for 2 days for a softer texture. To reconstitute, put cubes in soup kettle and carefully pour on boiling water. Pour off after 10 minutes. Then add lukewarm or cold water and press cakes gently between the palms to expel further liquid. Place cubes on paper towels and then transfer to lightly oiled baking sheet. For crisper exterior, roll lightly in arrowroot, potato starch or any pet powder (see index). Bake at 250°, turning occasionally, until cubes are brown and crisp. Cool. Store in refrigerator in plastic bags (add a cup of juice from The Gravy Bowl to moisten). Fidol is a snack, a supplement, a meal in itself.

Homemade Meow Mix

High-Protein, High-Fat, High-B-Vitamin Meal

ROLLED OATS   3 cups
WHEAT GERM or BRAN   1 cup
GRAIN (WHEAT, RYE, OATS, etc.)
    ½ cup, freshly ground
NUTS or SEEDS   1 cup, lightly toasted
BONE MEAL POWDER
    (HOMEMADE)   ¼ cup (see index)
DESICCATED LIVER POWDER   ¼ cup
BREWER'S YEAST   ¼ cup
KELP POWDER   1 teaspoon
VEGETABLE OIL   ¼ cup
ANY MUTT BUTTER   ½ cup melted (see index)
SOY MILK or WATER   ¼ cup (see index)

Mix dry ingredients well. Toss with oil, mutt butter, milk. Spread on lightly greased baking sheets and bake at 350° for 20 minutes. Turn often to brown well on all sides. Makes 8 cups of crunchy kibble. Store in airtight containers or freeze half in heavy-duty plastic sacks.

Cats require more protein and vitamin B than dogs or people.

Milk Bones

BARLEY FLOUR   1½ cups, freshly ground
HOMEMADE BONE MEAL
   POWDER   2 tablespoons (see index)
SEA SALT or KELP POWDER   ½ teaspoon
BAKING SODA   2 teaspoon
SHORTENING or FAT   1½ tablespoons
EGG YOLK   1
BUTTERMILK or SOY MILK   ½ cup (see index)
HONEY   2 tablespoons

Sift together dry ingredients; cream with melted fat.
Beat together yolk, milk, and honey; gradually add to
dry ingredient mixture. Knead into dough and turn out
onto floured board. Roll to about ½-inch thick and cut
into rectangular or bone-shaped biscuits; use kipper
can to cut out oval milk bones. Prick with fork. Put bones
on greased baking sheet and bake at 375° for about 20
minutes. Turn once to brown evenly.

Pupcorn

CORN ON THE COB   10 to 12 ears

Wrap ears of sweet corn in cheesecloth and dry in very
warm place—in the sun is ideal; a closet or attic is good,
too. (When corn is shriveled and dried, it is easy to
remove from cob.) Remove from cob and store in airtight jars. Eat as a crunchy snack,* rich in fiber.

*See Bowser By-product #1.

Mehitaballs
Meatless Meatballs for Kitty

DOGGEREL II   12 ounces (see index)
WALNUTS   ¼ cup shelled and chopped
ONION   ½, minced
HOUND BURGER HELPER I   ¼ cup (see index)
WHOLE EGG   1, lightly beaten
FRESH PET GREENS or PET
   GRASS   3 tablespoons, minced
MISO   4 teaspoons
OIL   for shallow frying

Combine all ingredients except oil. Mix well and shape into small balls. Heat oil in wok or skillet and sauté balls until browned on all sides, yet moist inside. Drain well and serve warm with Cat Catsup, of course.

Cat Catsup

VEGETABLE OIL   2 tablespoons
TOMATOES   2 pounds, cut in chunks
MEDIUM ONION   1, chopped
GREEN PEPPER   1, chopped
HONEY   1 tablespoon
LEMON JUICE   ¼ cup
SALT, KELP POWDER, and CLOVES   pinch of each

Grease large skillet; cook tomato and onion over medium heat until onion is transparent. Remove from heat and allow to cool. Put in blender and blend at low speed until smooth; add green pepper and blend in. Blend in remaining ingredients until quite smooth. Good on Mehitaballs. Hold the pickles!

All-Purpose Pet Soup

RICE POWER POWDER $^2/_3$ cup (see index)
FRESH or CANNED CARROT JUICE   24 ounces
BUTTER   2 tablespoons
BONE MEAL BROTH   enough to thin

Put power powder into heavy-bottomed pot or double boiler. Add carrot juice, a little at a time, and beat mixture with wire whisk. When juice and powder are well blended, add butter. Bring mixture to a boil over low heat (or boiling water if using double boiler), stirring constantly. Gradually stir in enough bone meal broth to thin to desired consistency and simmer 20 minutes, covered. Cool to lukewarm. Good with addition of small meatballs for a full-course meal.

Cream of Bone Soup

NECK BONES   1½ pounds
WATER
SOY MILK or BUTTERMILK   1 cup (see index)
PET GREENS POWER POWDER   2 tablespoons
    or more (see index)

Break bones into pieces that will fit inside mason jars. Pack bones in and fill with plenty of water. Close jars and process in pressure cooker at 10 to 12 pounds for 2 to 3 hours. The longer the bones cook and the higher the heat, the softer they will become. Put resulting soft bones into blender with milk and powder and blend into a creamy soup. Serve lukewarm in saucers or as gravy over regular meals. Good chow for dogs or cats.

Save leftovers for By-product #7.

Souper Bowl
Mutt's Marrowbone Soup

MARROWBONES   2 or 3
TURKEY DRUMSTICKS   1 or 2, skinned
VEGETABLE OIL   1 tablespoon
GARLIC CLOVE   1, chopped
LARGE ONION   1, coarsely chopped
CELERY STALKS and
  LEAVES   2, coarsely chopped
CARROTS   2 to 4, thickly sliced
LARGE TOMATO   1, chopped
WATER   about 6 cups
KELP POWDER   2 teaspoons

In stockpot, lightly brown bones and meat in oil. Add garlic and onion. Cover pot and simmer for 30 minutes. Add remaining ingredients. Bring to a boil, turn down to low simmer, and cook for several hours. Fortify with 1 or more tablespoons of any power powder (see index). Serve lukewarm or chilled to use for Bowser By-product #6. The magic of marrowbone resides in its rich nutritive protein for use in the body's own bones and tissues. A real tail-wagger!

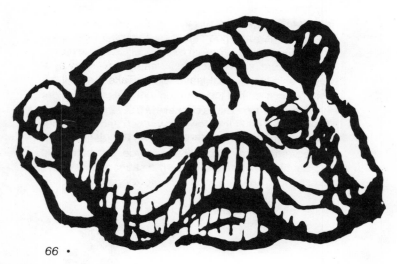

Bone-Less:

Dietary Doggerel

Pet got a potbelly? Here are some low-calorie formulas for reducing fat cats and paunchy pooches.

Slush Puppy Ice Cream

FREEZE-DRIED DECAFFEINATED
   COFFEE POWDER*   1 tablespoon
WATER   1 cup
NONFAT DRY MILK or
   SOY MILK POWDER   1 cup
VEGETABLE OIL   1 tablespoon
HONEY   2 tablespoons
VANILLA or ALMOND EXTRACT   1 teaspoon
KELP POWDER   ½ teaspoon

In deep bowl, blend coffee and water. Add remaining ingredients and whisk briefly. Put into freezer tray and freeze for about 1 hour; beat mixture and freeze for another 30 minutes. Repeat this procedure twice more. When mixture is very thick and creamy, cover tray and freeze until firm—for at least 1 hour. Take the chill off before serving. This ice cream is virtually calorie-free.

*Preferable to use homemade grain coffee powder or any herbal coffee powder (Postum is another possibility), available at health food stores.

Sugarless Dog Biscuits

Soft Pack

WHOLE EGGS   2
DATES   1 cup pitted
ANY MUTT BUTTER   ½ cup (see index)
CAROB POWDER   2 tablespoons
BONE MEAL POWDER
   (HOMEMADE)   1 cup (see index) or
   SOY MILK POWDER   1 cup

Combine eggs, dates, and mutt butter. Add carob and bone meal; mix well. Put into greased pan and bake at 325° until done. Biscuits will be soft. Cut into squares.

Hard Pack

KELP POWDER or SEA SALT   ½ teaspoon
DRY NATURAL SWEETENER   1 teaspoon
WHOLE-WHEAT FLOUR   2 cups
UNBLEACHED WHITE FLOUR   1 cup
LIVER POWDER   1 tablespoon
SOY MILK POWDER   1 cup
ANY MUTT BUTTER   ¹/₃ cup (see index)
MILK   ½ cup

Sift kelp and sweetener with both flours. Blend in liver powder, milk powder, and mutt butter. Add just enough milk to make very stiff dough. Knead on floured board until dough becomes soft and pliable. Run dough through meat grinder using coarse blade or mash with potato masher until smooth. Roll to ½-inch thickness. Cut with biscuit cutter, prick with fork, and bake in moderate oven (350°) for 30 minutes. Biscuits should be an appropriate bone color.

Muttrecal

YOGURT   1 cup
SOY MILK   2 cups (see index)
BREWER'S YEAST   1 teaspoon
KELP POWDER   ½ teaspoon
CAROB POWDER   1 tablespoon
SOY MILK POWDER   1 tablespoon
RAW WHEAT GERM or BRAN   1 tablespoon
EGG YOLK   1
VEGETABLE OIL   1 tablespoon
SPROUTS   1 tablespoon or more chopped
SEEDS   1 tablespoon toasted

Combine all ingredients and blend until smooth. Serve to any ever-hungry hound by the half-cup throughout the day.

Minus Milk

RENNET TABLET   ½ tablet
WATER   2 tablespoons, cold
LOW FAT or SKIM MILK   ½ gallon

Dissolve junket in water. Heat milk in deep kettle to approximately 86°. Remove from heat and stir in dissolved junket. Put kettle on asbestos pad or flame tamer over low flame or burner, cover, and wait until curd separates from whey (about 3 to 4 hours). Line colander with double thickness of cheesecloth and pour in curds and whey. Save curds to eat; pour whey into pan and cook until thicker and sweeter. Refrigerate and serve as a saucer-snack between meals. A half-milk made from whey minus most of milk's fat and calories.

Minus Milk Flakes

An Unsweetened Sweet for Fat Cats

MINUS MILK

Continue to heat thickened Minus Milk until reduced to
one-quarter of its former quantity. Spoon into pie pan
and set into low oven (125° to 200°) until dry and flaky.
As a bonus, it will be twice as sweet as before.

Diet Dog Dodgers

Mock Cornmeal Dog Biscuits

MILLET   1½ cups, finely ground
KELP POWDER   ¼ teaspoon
HOMEMADE BONE MEAL
   POWDER   ½ cup (see index)
VEGETABLE OIL   ⅙ cup
WATER   about 3 cups, boiling

Combine all ingredients except water. Then combine
boiling water with all other ingredients. When mixture is
cool, shape into small biscuits (add more flour or meal if
dough is too wet). Place on greased baking sheet and
bake at 350° for 20 minutes. Turn once to brown on both
sides. Makes about 12.

For a high-calorie, high-carbohydrate version, see
Doggie Dodgers.

Pet Vegechips

No Fat, No Frying

POTATO   1, well scrubbed, skin on, thinly sliced
SMALL EGGPLANT   ½, peeled and thinly sliced
SMALL GREEN or YELLOW SQUASH   1, thinly sliced
ANY WELL-FLAVORED DOG DIP or
    CAT NIP   about ½ cup

Dip sliced vegetables in cat nip or dog dip and marinate 15 minutes. Shake off excess liquid, place on
parchment baking paper or directly on ungreased
cookie sheet, and put into 150° oven. Oven-dry for 30
minutes. Turn oven off, leave door ajar, and let slices
dry out completely (this may be a several-day process
which you can speed along by repeating the heating
once daily). Chips are done when very dry and crispy.
Keep in tightly closed jar or canister.

Rin Tin Thins

Rye Wafers

WHOLE-RYE FLOUR   1 cup
WHOLE-WHEAT FLOUR   ½ cup
KELP POWDER   ¼ teaspoon
VEGETABLE OIL   2 tablespoons
WATER   4 tablespoons

Mix flours and kelp. Add oil and mix well. Add enough
water to give dough a kneading consistency. Knead for
5 minutes. Roll out dough to desired thinness and cut
into squares or circles with biscuit cutter. Prick with fork.
Place on greased cookie sheet; bake at 325° for 10 to
12 minutes.

Diet Pupsie

APPLE JUICE or CHERRY JUICE   1 cup
NATURALLY SPARKLING MINERAL WATER   1 cup

Combine and uncork on special occasions. Bowser deserves an occasional bit of the old bubbly, too!

Gain-Burgers
High-Calorie Chow Cakes for String Bean Spaniels, Puny Poodles, and Other "Slow Gainers"

GROUND MEAT or BOILED
   CHICKEN (boned)   1 pound
READY-TO-COOK CEREAL   1 cup
BROWN RICE   1 cup cooked
ANY POWER POWDER   ¼ cup (see index)
WHOLE EGGS   3, beaten
KELP POWDER   2 teaspoons
VEGETABLE OIL   2 tablespoons
CORNMEAL   1 cup
SHORTENING   ½ cup, melted
VEGETABLES   1 cup grated
HOMEMADE BROTH or SOY
   MILK   3 cups (see index)

For a loaf: Combine all ingredients thoroughly. Spoon into greased baking pans; bake at 350° for 1 hour. Cool. Cut into squares or crumble and store in refrigerator containers to mix with regular rations.

For burger patties: Combine all ingredients thoroughly, then shape into patties. Place on greased cookie sheet and bake about 35 minutes (or until done in the centers). Cool. Wrap in foil and put in freezer bags and freeze any patties not needed through the week.

Bone-Bone Bonbons:

Sweets and Treats

Mock Mutt Chocolates

Sugar-free and Chocolate-free Canine Caramels

    WATER   ½ cup, warm
    BUTTER or SOFT SHORTENING   2 tablespoons
    CAROB POWDER   ½ cup
    SOY MILK POWDER, POWDERED WHEY, or
       BONE MEAL POWDER   ⅓ cup (see index)
    SOY LECITHIN GRANULES*   2 tablespoons
    DRIED FRUIT   1 cup diced
    PEANUTS   1 cup shelled with skins

In blender, mix together water, butter, carob powder milk powder, and lecithin granules until smooth. Put fruit and nuts in bowl and pour carob mixture over them; mix well until every piece is coated. Lightly grease large baking sheet. Spoon out teaspoonfuls of mixture in clusters. Put cookie sheet into cold oven on middle rack. Bake at 300° for 10 to 15 minutes until tops are dry. Remove sheet and let chocolates dry thoroughly.

*A natural emulsifier. Turns out a smooth and nutritious chocolate sauce.

Paws and Claws
Doggie Danish

BUTTER   ½ cup
VEGETABLE OIL   ½ cup
WHOLE-GRAIN FLOUR   1 cup
BAKING YEAST   2 tablespoons
SOY MILK or WATER   2 cups, scalded and cooled
  (see index)
HONEY   2 tablespoons
SALT or KELP POWDER   ½ teaspoon
LEMON JUICE   1 teaspoon
WHOLE-WHEAT FLOUR   5½ cups
DATE SUGAR   ⅓ cup
ANY MUTT BUTTER   for spread (see index)
HONEY, and WATER, or EGG YOLK   for glaze

MIXTURE I: Cream butter and oil with whole-grain flour until well blended. Chill 30 to 40 minutes.
MIXTURE II: Dissolve yeast in soy milk. Add honey and let proof for 10 minutes. Add salt and lemon juice to Mixture II. Stir in 2 cups whole-wheat flour and beat until smooth and elastic. Let rise 20 minutes in warm place, then beat in sugar and remaining flour.
Turn out dough on lightly floured board and knead until firm. Roll dough into ½-inch thick rectangle. Put mixture I on half the dough and fold over other half of dough to encase it. Press lightly and fold the right hand third of dough over center third. Then fold left hand third over center. Roll dough out to 1-inch thickness. Fold over again. Roll and repeat this rolling and folding 4 more times. Roll into a rectangle ½-inch thick and spread with mutt butter. Roll left and right sides towards the center (forming paws and claws) and carefully slice off inch-thick slices with sharp knife. If slicing is difficult, chill dough another 30 minutes and try again. Place paws and claws on greased cookie sheet and let rise for 30 minutes. Bake at 375° for 15 minutes. When partially cooled, glaze with honey and water or beaten egg yolk.

Good-Dog Goodbars

DRY MILK POWDER   ½ cup
SOY MILK POWDER   ½ cup
ANY POWER POWDER   1 to 2 tablespoons
  (see index)
EGG WHITE   1, whipped with a fork
BLACKSTRAP or UNSULFURED
  MOLASSES   4 or more tablespoons

Combine all powders (sift for smoother texture). Add egg white and then molasses, a drop at a time. When you have a very soft but no longer sticky dough (if sticky, firm up with cornstarch or arrowroot powder), press into lightly buttered rectangular dish, using fingers to pack firmly; chill until stiff. Cut into bars and dispense as treats. Makes about 24 candies.

Canine Whipped Cream
Low-Cost Coconut Dessert

COCONUT   2 cups fresh shredded* or unsweetened
  packaged shredded
ALMOND PASTE   4 tablespoons
COCONUT MILK or WATER   as needed
VANILLA EXTRACT   1 teaspoon

Put coconut into blender with almond paste. Add enough coconut milk to liquefy. Add vanilla and liquefy until smooth like whipped cream. Serve like pudding whenever the sweet tooth must be served—whether two-footed or four-footed.

*To prepare fresh coconut, freeze whole nut. Pound open with hammer (reserve the chunks of frozen milk to eat as an ice cream dessert); cut off brown hull and cut coconut meat into small chunks. Shred in blender.

Almond Bark
Sugarless Canine Candy

HONEY   1 cup
ALMONDS   1 to 1½ cups slivered or sliced
KELP POWDER or ANY
    POWER POWDER   pinch (see index)

In medium-sized saucepan cook honey over very low heat until it tests at the "hardball" stage. Lightly grease two 7½ x 3½-inch baking pans. Spread shelled nuts over bottom of pans; add kelp powder to honey; then pour honey over nuts. (Don't wait for foam to settle; bubbles help to make candy lighter.) Spread honey into corners. Allow candy to cool completely. Spread sheet of wax paper over flat surface, invert candy pans over paper and rap pan sharply a couple of times until sheets of brittle come free. Break into about 50 pieces of dandy doggie candy.

Pooch Pudding
High-Protein Puppy Parfait

WHOLE EGGS   2, hard-cooked
VERY RIPE BANANAS   2, peeled
COTTAGE CHEESE   1 cup or
    DOGGEREL II   1 cup, scrambled (see index)
LEMON JUICE   2 tablespoons
HONEY   1 tablespoon

Cut each egg in half slicing right through shell and scooping out contents into blender. Add bananas; whir until smooth; add remaining ingredients and blend again until smooth and fluffy. Pour into large soup bowl and chill until firm. Bring to room temperature before serving. Serves 6 puppies.

Catsanjammer Jam
Uncooked Fruit Kibble for Kitty's Toast

DRIED DATES, APRICOTS or OTHER
   DRIED FRUIT   1 cup, pitted
ANY POWER POWDER or WHEAT
   GERM   2 tablespoons (see index)
HONEY or FRUIT JUICE   a bit

Do not chop or soak fruit. Feed it through food grinder
using blade with medium-sized holes. Fruit will emerge
like spaghetti strands. Sprinkle strands with power
powder and mash with spoon, moistening with bit of
honey or fruit juice, according to pussy's preference.
Store in sterilized jelly jars. Spread on bits of cracker or
toast.

Cat Krispies
Mock Popcorn for the Family Cat

WATER or HOMEMADE BROTH   2 cups
NATURAL BROWN RICE   1 cup
KELP POWDER   1½ teaspoons

Bring water to a boil in small, heavy pot. Stir in rice and
kelp. Bring to a boil again, then lower heat and simmer
uncovered 35 to 45 minutes, until tender but still slightly
chewy. There should be no water left in pan. Spread out
cooked rice on cookie sheet or in roasting pan. Bake in
400° oven for 30 minutes, stirring at 10-minute intervals.
When rice is golden brown and tends to clump, remove
from oven. A good crackly nibble. Can be made with
leftover rice, too.

Super Fudge for Super Cats

POWDERED SOY MILK or
   POWDERED SKIM MILK   ½ cup
COCOA or CAROB POWDER   ¼ cup
GROUND NUTS or SPROUT
   POWER POWDER   ¼ cup
HONEY   ¼ cup
MUTT BUTTER II   ¼ cup (see index)
COARSE BRAN   1 cup
BREWER'S YEAST   2 tablespoons
DRIED FRUIT   ½ cup, minced
SOY OIL   as needed

Combine all ingredients except oil in large mixing bowl. Mix with your fingers until thoroughly combined. Add oil bit by bit until mixture has proper fudgelike consistency. Press mixture into greased pan and chill until fairly firm. Cut into 3 x 3-inch squares.

# Beyond the Bone:

Cosmetics and Remedies

Canine Coat Conditioner

    COARSE BRAN   1 cup
    WATER   4 cups, cold
    HERBAL SHAMPOO   2 ounces
    EGG YOLKS   2
    WATER   1 cup, warm

Pour bran into cold water. Bring to a boil and simmer for 5 minutes. Strain through gauze or cheesecloth and add shampoo. Beat eggs with warm water, add to shampoo mixture. Massage mixture into coat covering each hair. Rinse out with tepid water. Massage coat well with thick turkish towel. Hair! Hair!

Cat's Coat Thickener

    ROSEMARY FLOWERS   1 handful
    RAW HONEY   ½ pound
    WHITE WINE   1 quart
    SWEET ALMOND OIL   ¼ pint

Mix rosemary with honey and wine. Distill mixture. Add oil and shake well. To use, pour small amount into cup, warm it, and rub into cat's coat, right down to the roots. Plain rosemary tea also seems to be effective as a coat thickener. An age-old remedy for thinning hair.

Body Oil for After Bath

SESAME OIL   1 tablespoon
WHEAT GERM OIL   1 tablespoon
AVOCADO OIL   1 tablespoon
SCENT(from FLAVORING EXTRACTS,
   SPICES, or DRIED HERBS)   as desired

Mix all ingredients together. Massage your pet's coat and skin thoroughly with oil. May also be used heated. Good for pet's coat or psyche.

See Bowser By-product #10.

Hot Oil Conditioner

CASTOR OIL   2 tablespoons
OLIVE OIL   2 tablespoons

Warm oils together in top of double boiler. When they reach temperature that is comfortable to use, remove from heat and apply directly to scalp and hair. Massage your pet's coat with the warmed oils and "steam" them under hot towels for as long as your pet can be coaxed to sit still. Shampoo thoroughly after towels are off.

Dry Pet's Penicillin

To aromatize your pet's meal, bury 1 or 2 cloves of peeled garlic under several cups of dry ration and keep sack or container tightly closed for a few hours. Garlic-scented food stimulates appetites.

Simple Oil Shampoo

SULFONATED OLIVE OIL*   2 tablespoons
SULFONATED CASTOR OIL*   2 tablespoons
DISTILLED WATER   ½ cup
HERBS or SPICES   as desired
FOOD COLORING   for tint, if desired

Stir together until well blended. Bottle up. Rinse well after shampooing.

*See Sources for Mail-Order Supplies.

Pet's Penicillin

WATER   1 quart
GARLIC CLOVES   12 to 20
FRESH PARSLEY   1 tablespoon chopped
SAGE   ¼ teaspoon
THYME   ¼ teaspoon
WHOLE CLOVE   1
BAY LEAF   1
VEGETABLE OIL   2 tablespoons

Combine all ingredients and bring to a boil. Reduce heat, cover, and simmer for 30 minutes. Serve as bracing between-meal tonic or serve over kitty's semimoist or dry dinner. (Garlic need not be eaten raw. It is, in fact, sweeter stewed like this.)

Dental Powder for Dogs and Cats

CALCIUM CARBONATE*   1¾ teaspoons
MAGNESIUM CARBONATE*   1 teaspoon
POWDERED DATE SUGAR   ¾ teaspoon
SODIUM PERBORATE*   ½ teaspoon
NEUTRAL WHITE SOAP POWDER*   ¼ teaspoon
FLAVORING (from NATURAL HERBS
   and SPICES)   as desired

Put everything except flavoring into mortar and crush well. Slowly add flavoring and continue to crush until evenly mixed. Makes ⅛ cup.

*See Sources for Mail-Order Supplies.

Dental Paste for Pets

MILK OF MAGNESIA   5 teaspoons
CALCIUM CARBONATE*   3¼ teaspoons
WHITE POWDERED SOAP   ¼ teaspoon
GUM TRAGACANTH*   ¼ teaspoon
GLYCERIN*   about 2 teaspoons
DISTILLED WATER   2 teaspoons
CRYSTALLIZED HONEY   1 teaspoon
MINERAL OIL   ¼ teaspoon
FLAVORING (NATURAL HERBS, SPICES)   as desired

Grind dry ingredients in mortar, mixing well. Add liquids and mix until paste is smooth. Makes ¼ cup.

*See Sources for Mail-Order Supplies.

The Mutt Medic

Mutt Medic I

Make Your Mutt Feel Better with Butter

Miso (used in Mutt Butter VI) has long been known in the Orient as a wonder food for all creatures. Providing easily assimilated protein and essential minerals in a "cup-a-soup" form, miso is buttery, rich, slightly salty-tasting soybean paste with a friendly bacteria that helps digest other foods and supplies glucose for stamina and energy.

Mutt Medic II

Mastiff Digestif–One Way

PAPAYA   1
LEMON or LIME JUICE   2 teaspoons
CAROB POWDER   optional

Peel and seed papaya. Cut into chunks and purée in blender. Add lemon juice. Pour into refrigerator tray to jell. Cut into cubes and roll in sifted carob powder. Try 1 or 2 cubes as a mutt-gut-get-better.

The papaya contains an enzyme that digests protein and therefore stimulates digestion.

Mutt Medic III

Look to—
the coconut for a worm-free Weimaraner: "Desiccated or fresh-grated coconut is enjoyed; it supplies vital albumen and also expels worms," says herbal veterinarian Juliette de Bairacli-Levy.

or to—
the Gravenstein for a glossy-coated pussy. A tablespoon of apple cider vinegar mixed into kitty's supper each day works wonders, say herbalists.

Mutt Medic IV
How to Help a Fat Cat!

Fiber is your friend. Replace some of the carbohydrate and fat in puss's regular fare with bran. Rather than dishing up everything in more petite portions, this method will provide your pet with an adequate amount of protein, vitamins, and minerals while reducing calories.

Mutt Medic V
Some Old-fashioned Natural Home Remedies

*Antiparasitic preventive medicine: lots of raw and cooked greens, liver, and dried apricots.

*Flea dispenser: ¼ teaspoon cider vinegar a day in puss's water dish for 3 days.

*Worm-away I: generous nibblings of catnip, sorrel, hyssop, vervain, and chamomile leaves.

*Worm-away II: garlic buds and pumpkin seeds before bedtime and castor oil the next day.

Appendixes

Sources for Mail-Order Supplies

Erewhon Natural Foods 33 Farnsworth Street Boston, MA 02210	whole grains, flours, seaweed, cereals, oils, wide variety of natural foodstuffs
Walnut Acres Penns Creek, PA 17862	general health food store, as above
Van Waters & Rogers P.O. Box 3200 San Francisco, CA 94119	cosmetic and grooming aid supplies
Committee on Animal Nutrition National Academy of Sciences 2101 Constitution Avenue, NW Washington, D.C. 20418	information on pet food diets
Petpower Products Kissimmee, FL 32741	pet food supplements
Rocky Hollow Herb Farm Box 215 Lake Wallkill Rd. Sussex, NJ 07461	herbs and spices of all kinds
The Smilie Company 575 Howard Street San Francisco, CA 94105	dried greens, dried fish, and other dehydrated foods

IS IT FACT OR FICTION THAT . . .

1. both dogs and people have higher protein requirements than cats?
2. crippling arthritis in cats may be the result of excessive feeding of fresh liver?
3. vitamin C (ascorbic acid) is not necessary as a dietary supplement for cats and dogs?
4. too much meat or straight meat will produce diarrhea in most puppies and some dogs?
5. the incidence of diabetes is about 10 percent for both cat and dog populations in this country?
6. feeding excess amounts of red tuna fish can lead to severe Vitamin E deficiency?
7. the most common nutritional deficiency in cats is steatitis?
8. hyperthyroidism in animals is caused by too much carbohydrate?
9. a cat can live well on 300 to 400 calories a day?
10. a cat on a steady diet of canned fish is not getting enough calcium and ash?
11. a puppy should get 100 calories per pound of body weight a day?
12. feline digestive juices are not as rich in ptyalin as those of humans; therefore they do not digest starches as efficiently as their owners?
13. dogs over the age of eight months require 50 percent fewer calories and half as much protein as puppies?
14. a big bowl of milk every day prevents the formation of kidney stones in cats?
15. voluminous stools following the feeding of certain brands of dog foods indicate that they probably contain too much fiber and should be discontinued?
16. fasting one day a week is beneficial for both dogs and puppies?

ANSWERS to the above on the following page.

Answers to Paws

1. No, the opposite is true.
2. True.
3. True, they manufacture their own.
4. True.
5. True.
6. Yes, true.
7. True.
8. False. Too much phosphorus and too little calcium.
9. Yes.
10. False. He is getting too much.
11. Yes.
12. True.
13. Fact.
14. False. It can have the opposite effect.
15. True, but it may also contain very low-grade ingredients. Discontinue use in either case.
16. True.

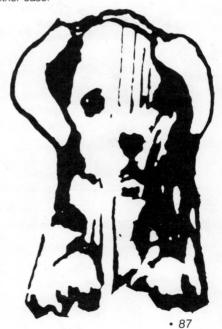

The Dog Pound I

LESS THAN 50 CALORIES
1   cup mung bean sprouts 30
1   cup soybean sprouts 46
1   ounce soy flour 30
1   teaspoon soy sauce 10
1   tablespoon blackstrap molasses 45
1   cup fresh watercress 10
1   tablespoon miso 24

LESS THAN 100 CALORIES
4   tablespoons carob powder 51
1   slice whole-wheat bread 55
½   cup bean curd (tofu) 80
¼   cup raisins 80
1   ounce sunflower seeds 86
2   tablespoons brewer's yeast 50
1   tablespoon soy lecithin granules 60
½   cup coconut meal 76

LESS THAN 200 CALORIES
¼   cup desiccated liver powder 120
¼   cup wheat germ 110
1   cup plain yogurt 130
¼   cup sesame seeds 140
1   cup bran flour 150
½   cup cashews or almonds 140
¼   cup honey 168
2   tablespoons unrefined oil 200
1   cup dry dates 178

WORKING OFF WHAT TOWSER AND TABBY EAT

INPUT	OUTPUT
½ cup unsweetened applesauce	2 minutes on the run
1 plain dog biscuit	78-minute snooze for Snoopy
1 4-ounce slice meat loaf	30 minutes of brisk walking
1 bowl skim milk	fast 4-minute mouse chase
1 hard-cooked egg	50-minute catnap
1 raw carrot	run to the nearest tree and back
1 ounce butter	45-minute constitutional for the cat
1 small serving Grranola (or commercial versions)	2-hour dog nap
2 strips of bacon	18 minutes of aerobic dog walking
1 tablespoon crunchy peanut butter	74 minutes of transcendental muttitation

NEARLY NO CALORIES (but nutritionally high-powered)
Parsley, watercress, celery, zucchini, broccoli, most pet greens.

A TABLE OF SCRAPS: WHAT AND WHAT NOT TO PUT INTO THE KITTY, PUPPY, AND FAMILY DOG

Raw fish . . . . A definite no-no. It destroys vitamin B_1 and can lead to heart disease, paralysis.

Lamb and pork scraps . . . . Good protein but probable unhealthy amounts of fat.

Soups . . . . If not overly salty, too hot, or too cold. Note: Brothlike soups sometimes have a laxative effect on pets.

Pork sausage, bacon . . . . Too much salt, too much fat, too much seasoning. A no-no.

Purely starchy foods, e.g., potatoes, and watery vegetables . . . . Poorly digested by feline and canine alike.

Raw eggs . . . . Yolks yes, whites in moderation (they destroy the important B-vitamin biotin).

Tomatoes . . . . Fermentative for many pets. Avoid unless your pet demonstrates a fondness and tolerance.

Raw liver/cooked liver . . . . The former causes diarrhea in some cats and the latter may constipate. Find a happy medium. This is a super-valuable food.

Corn . . . . Must be well cooked, well sprouted, or well ground and heated for proper digestion.

Bowser By-products

1. More Pupcorn than your snack jar will hold? Grind it into a delicious toasted corn flour or a "sprinkle" for any canned meal.

2. Make Towser patties with ½ pound leftover Doggerel II, 3 chopped green onions, 1 teaspoon caraway seeds, 1 large grated carrot, 2 tablespoons brewer's yeast, 1 teaspoon raw wheat germ. Shape into small cakes and cook 10 minutes on each side in 350° oven.

3. Make some yeast fudge. Not sweet, not fattening, but supernutritious. Toast ¾ cup brewer's yeast lightly in low oven until golden; stir into ⅓ cup melted shortening or butter with wire whisk. Add ¼ cup bone meal powder, ½ teaspoon garlic powder, 1 teaspoon kelp powder, and small amount of water or soy milk to make thickish paste. Press into square candy dish pregreased and scattered with cornmeal, and freeze. Thaw a bit; chop into nuggets. Superstar snack.

4. Turn ½ cup Hound Burger Helper I into cat or dog yummies. Mix bran flakes with a bit of apple juice, add very finely minced dried fruit bits. Press down hard and divide up into little snack nuggets.

5. Leftover Seviche? Make fish jerky. Soak fish in soy sauce for 1 hour. Drain, cut into small strips, and hang from spokes of cake or oven rack. Place rack in oven over pan to catch drippings, and "dry roast" overnight in warm (100° to 125°) oven. Keeps indefinitely. Store in glass jars.

6. Chill any leftover Souper Bowl and presto, you have pet jello. Or freeze what is left in ice cube trays and use a cube at a time when you need a quick broth.

7. Leftover Cream of Bone Soup can be refrigerated to produce liver-flavored pet jello. Slice and serve by the sliver as a 'tween-meal eat.

8. Too much Gravy Grains gravy? Make yourself a delicious cup of 100 percent natural decaffeinated coffee. Use 6 ounces of fresh water and 2 tablespoons Gravy Grains powder for each cup of coffee. Process as usual in your coffee maker.

9. Pet Greens Pasta in its uncooked and uncut state can be turned into a pea green pie shell. Roll a bit thinner than for noodles, press into a small, pregreased casserole dish, trim and flute edges, and prick here and there. Bake 20 minutes at

350°. Cool, remove from dish, wrap, and freeze until you need it for your or your dog's next stew.

10. Should not dog's best friend share in some of his grooming finery? A little bit of this body lotion makes a most luxurious manhandler's hand lotion.

11. Pour leftover applesauce over a large square of clear plastic wrap and spread very thinly using a rubber spatula. Put into a 150° oven for 30 minutes. Turn oven off, leave oven door slightly ajar, and let the spread slowly turn into a nice, firm, chewy "apple leather" (count on several days for the transformation).

Index